Notes To My Boy

Darling Amy

Lots of love

J. Smith

xxx

Notes To
My Boy

Jo
Swallow

Matador
9 Priory Business Park,
Wistow Road, Kibworth Beauchamp,
Leicestershire. LE8 0RX
Tel: 0116 279 2299
Email: books@troubador.co.uk
Web: www.troubador.co.uk/matador
Twitter: @matadorbooks

ISBN 978 1789015 089

British Library Cataloguing in Publication Data.
A catalogue record for this book is available from the British Library.

Typeset in 11pt Gill Sans by Troubador Publishing Ltd, Leicester, UK

Matador is an imprint of Troubador Publishing Ltd

Thank you, Tom, for gifting me Teddy -
my love for you both grows every day.

Contents

Introduction

Poems written to my son. A reflection on the first eighteen months of motherhood. The joy, the fear and everything in between.

Becoming a Mum releases a love like never before. Your child becomes your world and it is hard to remember how life was before they came along. The magic of holding them in your arms is unbeatable. For me it has been an incredible journey, but it is only just beginning. Already along the way I have been shocked at how hard it is to keep going through the toughest of days, amazed at how the process of bringing up a child blows your mind and surprised at how much your life changes in every single way.

These poems are written to capture my emotions of being a new Mum. I hope others can relate to, laugh with, cry at or just enjoy my writing.

First Impressions

long fingers
closed eyes
tiny toes
skinny thighs

no hair
button nose
flaky hands
pouting pose

full lips
soft skin
peaceful face
slight grin

sharp nails
heart ticks
straight back
leg kicks

little whimper
scrunched fist
cute hiccups
endless list

Up and Out

The midwife says take a shower,
To eat up the toast she made,
Drink up the hot tea,
The bed needs to be re-laid,

I really think she is joking,
I'm stitched up to the max,
I can't possibly move,
Surely its time to relax,

But no, she is being serious,
I must get on with it,
No time like the present,
Not a moment to just sit,

Off the bed I try to roll,
Not able to stand up right,
No choice but to carry on,
Find strength with all my might,

I am a real life mum now,
No space or time to rest,
This world is just beginning,
Off I go to do my best.

The Early Days

I don't even attempt to put you down
As you sleep on my chest all the time
Watching you breathe is magical
I still can't believe you are mine.

The birth was horrid in every way
I struggle to even think clearly
But seeing your perfect face in the light
Makes my heart pound ever so dearly.

You make everything better
From sleepless nights at the start
The hardest of days become lighter
As I listen to the beat of your heart.

Are you really my baby?
A son to call my own
How could this miracle have happened?
Just look how we have grown.

Through tears and clouds of darkness
Long days and longer nights
Your lips and eyes and hands
Are the most delicate of sights.

Thank you for showing me the way
When all I could see was fear
We will be ok my boy
Of that you have made it clear.

Up All Night

Being up all night was a different thing
Before you came along
Being up all night had a different feel
Meant dancing to a song.

Being up all night was once a week
Before I was a Mum
Chilling at a house party
Drinking my coke and rum.

Being up all night was 'til two o'clock
Not really all night at all
Dancing in a grotty club
With the odd drunken fall!

Being up all night was free and easy
Not rocking you to sleep
Partying with my best mates
And giggling in a heap.

Being up all night had a different meaning
Not feeding you a lot
Dancing on the beach in summer
Getting nice and hot.

Being up all night was manageable
When it was now and then
When I was younger and full of beans
I could do it again and again.

What If I get It Wrong?

What if I get it wrong one day
What if I let you down
What if I say something incorrect
What if you see me frown

How do I keep you safe and warm
How do I shelter your eyes
How do I protect you from everything
How do I escape grey skies

When do I let you go free alone
When do I stop holding tight
When do I take the next big step
When do I let you take flight

The future is overwhelming
Far too much to bear
So for now we shall do our best
Knowing the love we share

The Washing Pile

No one tells you this side of things
The amount of washing a baby brings,
It's endless from the day they arrive
I'm amazed my machine is still alive.

No one tells you this side of things
The amount of washing a baby brings,
How can something so tiny wee
Get through clothes so ferociously.

No one tells you this side of things
The amount of washing a baby brings,
Three outfits per day and tons of socks
I daren't even look in my laundry box.

No one tells you this side of things
The amount of washing a baby brings,
When weaning starts the bibs come along
The pile grows more and more full on.

No one tells you this side of things
The amount of washing a baby brings,
It goes on and on every single day
If I close my eyes will it go away?

Relentless

I only fed you just now,
changed your nappy three times,
walked you round the block again,
sang you nursery rhymes.

Here we go all over again,
another feed and nappy,
we are on round five of the day,
in order to keep you happy.

I'm told it gets much easier,
as the early days are long,
the same thing over and over,
unsure if I'm getting it wrong.

We have walked for miles this morning,
to keep the tears at bay,
now it's the evening tricky patch,
just coming into play.

We somehow get through it all,
whilst drinking cold cups of tea,
AM I THE ONLY ONE STRUGGLING?
THIS NEW LIFE IS CHALLENGING ME.

Holding You

Watching the sun setting over the sea,
running along the river feeling free,
walking up mountains big and small,
holding you beats it all.

Eating pancakes on a quiet Sunday,
a glass of wine at the end of a Monday,
watching snowflakes flutter and fall,
holding you beats it all.

Favourite movie on a Friday night,
watching swans taking flight,
old friend's catch up call,
holding you beats it all.

Summer holidays in the sun,
dancing, drinking, endless fun,
swimming in a nice warm pool,
holding you beats it all.

Winter turning into spring,
birds start the day as they sing,
watching night time upon us fall,
holding you beats it all.

Sleep

Six months old and you slept right through,
felt like Christmas and my birthday too,
wow, I was shattered in so many ways,
but then I slept for what appeared like days,
it felt like forever to get to that point,
we were all in it together totally joint,
tired, grumpy and ulcers galore,
at one point I passed out on the kitchen floor,
but you cracked it eventually baby boy,
we are now all rested and jumping for joy.

Broken

There was a stage when I was broken,
can't even remember when,
like a murky blur for a while,
shed tears again and again,
I couldn't figure it out,
why I was feeling blue
with you in my world now,
my dreams had all come true.

But the shock of all the pain,
the tired and aching parts,
had left me in a quandary,
I didn't know where to start,
no time to put my body back,
and take some recovery,
rest was not an option,
being a mum was now me,
I felt so lost and alone,
not sure which way to turn,
but as the weeks unfolded,
I met mums that felt the burn.

Some glide through this journey,
for others it's not that smooth,
the biggest lesson I have learnt,
we all have nothing to prove,
the broken days don't last long,
but they get you into the swing,
of all the hurdles up ahead,
that motherhood does bring.

Opinions

Oh dear he has just fallen over
Oh dear he still can't talk
Oh dear he is crying a lot
Oh dear he has an odd walk

Oh dear he is eating chocolate
Oh dear he won't eat his lunch
Oh dear he's got the wrong spoon
Oh dear he is sat with a hunch

Oh dear he is rather loud
Oh dear he doesn't like eggs
Oh dear he gets a bit shy sometimes
Oh dear he has very long legs

The verdicts from others kill me,
Leave us alone, it's a pain
We are doing fine without these views
All the opinions drive me insane!

The Mum in Me

I never thought it would be like this,
so incredibly hard to cope,
to keep up with your beating heart
and not slip down a slope.

But you turned my world around,
for our little family of three
is getting stronger by the day
as we build dreams happily.

I never thought it would be this hard,
to stop the endless worry,
the fear, the anxiety, all the stress
for that little one I'm sorry.

But you changed everything for the good,
you made me stop and stand,
you make the world much better
when we walk hand in hand.

I never thought I would be so upset,
at the thought of not getting it right,
you are everything to me now,
each day a daunting sight.

But you saved me on the darkest days
I'm getting there my son,
you sort my head when it's in a mess
and the best is yet to come.

You and Your Daddy

When the working week is over,
the chaos slows down a lot,
nothing makes my heart burst more,
than when Daddy gets you from the cot.

I lie there listening to you chat,
I giggle at the laughter too,
it makes me feel so happy,
that you boys are mine right through.

My back gets a rest all day today,
arms free from straining so hard,
Daddy's got you covered boy,
as he chases you round the yard.

Team of three in the house right now,
more hands between us all,
another head to give ideas,
new games with bat and ball.

I just sit and watch the two of you,
he holds you in one arm,
protecting you in the safest way,
and free from any harm.

I feel proud to see you together,
when you laugh and run and play
there's nothing I'd rather watch,
than this bond I see today.

The Best Keeps Getting Better

Today was the best day ever:
you climbed the stairs on your own
across the room a ball was thrown
you used my slipper as a phone
and knew which door was our home

Today was the best day ever:
you said a new word today
you watched the ducks sail away
chatting to them I heard you say
quack quack, you wanted them to play

Today was the best day ever:
you cuddled me when I was low
you walked fast and walked slow
understood how to stop and go
my love for you will always grow

Today was the best day ever:
today topped the day before
as you learnt how to knock on next door's door
your little smiles lift everyone more,
what's around the corner to explore?

Buses and Ducks

Your two favourite things are buses and ducks as
   we pass them every day,
"Bus!" you shout, as they zoom down the road
   with never a single delay,
shiny and red and full of people, you wave and
   smile with such pride,
hoping that you get a wave back and one day
   perhaps take a ride,
and as for the ducks, you are hooked by their
   quack,
their shimmering colours of green, white and
   black,
they grab scraps of bread from your tiny wee
   hand
and scrabble and climb from the water to land,
oh, the littlest things make you happy my boy
and I watch you with awe as your face fills with
   joy.

The Snack Battle

Before I had a baby, I saw it as so wrong,
to give out snacks to them in order to get along,
I'll never do that, I said to myself each time,
when I'm a mum snacks will of course be a crime,
but how wrong I was with those very thoughts
as getting you in a buggy now takes all sorts,
a rice cake, an apple, a fruit bar or drink,
whatever keeps you busy so I can think,
its a game I play just to win you round,
as there's a top I want to buy in a shop I found
more crackers you would like, well yes you may,
if it gives me five minutes to browse the display,
I'm no keen shopper but when living in holes,
the odd new item is one of my mum goals,
so, heading into town when you want to
    roam free,
takes a buggy bribe most days, often sugary,
healthy, I try, but that doesn't always work,
as behind the banana, the KitKats lurk,
it's a battle I have each time I do this,
do I give into choccy for silent bliss?
but at the end of the day, you're growing up
    great,
the banana and chocolate are both first rate,

at giving me the odd bit of time to do,
a bit of me stuff, even go to the loo,
so, I'm sorry for judging Mums in the past,
snacks are winners, and long may they last.

Laying the Fire

It's winter time and pretty cold,
it's time to light the fire,
Daddy sits you on his knee,
as he builds the logs up higher.

You run and fetch the kindling,
helping Daddy all the way,
golden flames flare up,
we won't go cold today.

It's your special thing to do,
whilst Mummy has a bath,
make the room all cosy
and lie next to the hearth.

Creating memories in our home
it's simple but oh so sweet,
building fires with Daddy,
is the highlight of your week.

Us

We swim, we walk,
we play, we talk,
with many other tots,
but generally it's the two of us
roaming all the shops.

We laugh, we cry,
we sing, we try,
with lots of other mates,
but most of the time its the two of us
clambering over gates.

We dance, we cuddle,
we jump in a puddle,
with our friendly crew,
but a lot of the time its the two of us
together ploughing through.

We eat, we drink,
we sit and think,
at times we drift away,
because of you, we are now a two
teamed up to face each day.

The Big Wide World of Parenting

We all do it differently
we all have our style
we all get lost from time to time
we can sometimes take a while

as parents we are in it together
as Mums and Dads we grow
as each day can have its battles
as cracks can often show

there is no fight for who is best
there is no right or wrong
there are so many ways to raise them
there are ways to get along

we don't know each other's stories
we don't know behind closed doors
we don't know the trouble others have
we don't judge each other's flaws

Mums and Dads can mess it up
Mums and Dads can crumble
Mums and Dads are only human
Mums and Dads may tumble

we do our best every day
we can lend a smile to others
we may see sadness sometimes
we must unite as brothers

In it as one, is the kindest way
in it together we stand
in it to pick each other up
in it to lend a hand

so...

for when all is said and done
and our children are asleep in bed
we can breathe the day away
knowing we have kept them fed,
and their happy little faces,
dream exciting dreams,
and we as parents should be proud,
though it may not always be as it seems,
the days of illness or testing tempers
can be the hardest of all
but showing that love does outshine
any trough or fall.
it's a tough old game this crazy world
but worth many a strain
to see them growing daily
and dancing in the rain.

What Will You Be My Boy?

I look at you all the time and wonder what's
    your path,
your love of nature, cheeky smile and dainty
    little laugh,
creative mind and nimble fingers busy all day
    long,
running to the tv as soon as you hear a good
    song.
I think you will be a painter but maybe you'll
    be a vet,
but then of course your love of planes means
    flying jumbo jets.
I have no idea where you will head, but it's fun
    to try and guess
the roads in life you will take, the buttons you
    will press.
The mistakes you'll learn from but bounce
    right back,
all the places you will find when you veer off
    track,
what will you be my little man, it's on my mind
    all day,
your future is bright my darling, let nothing
    block your way.

I'm Still Me

My journey into motherhood sent me a little
    bit mad,
I didn't think I could still be me, which made
    me very sad.

I thought there were two different people
    inside my crazy head,
One side of me was Mummy and the other
    was Jo, I said.

I wasn't sure if I could be both depending on
    the crowd,
I kind of acted in two ways: shy Mum or Jo
    who's loud.

It wasn't until a dear friend said; *to us, you are
    always Jo,*
That I realised I'm still me as one, not giving
    two a go.

Underneath new lessons learnt and change
    in pace of life
I'm still the kind and loving friend, and happily
    married wife.

The Mum I am is just Jo but with more to
    share and to give,
Me but so much stronger; living a life I'm
    proud to live.

Lightning Source UK Ltd.
Milton Keynes UK
UKHW02f1629010818
326627UK00007B/244/P